Original title:
Propagating Love

Copyright © 2025 Creative Arts Management OÜ
All rights reserved.

Author: George Mercer
ISBN HARDBACK: 978-1-80581-915-8
ISBN PAPERBACK: 978-1-80581-442-9
ISBN EBOOK: 978-1-80581-915-8

Threads of Togetherness

In a world of tangled strings,
We laugh as the chaos sings,
Knitting hearts with odd-shaped yarn,
In this craft, we can't be worn.

Bumpy stitches, twists and turns,
With each loop, our passion burns,
We weave a quilt, oh what a sight,
Two silly hearts, in pure delight.

Cultivating Heartfelt Journeys

Two garden gnomes, side by side,
With shovels ready, full of pride,
We dig in soil, both rich and weird,
Planting laughter, as we cheered.

Compost dreams rise high in scent,
Every seed sown, a silly rant,
Watering jokes, oh what a mess,
In this patch, joy's our success.

The Garden of Us

In our plot of vibrant blooms,
We dance in sunshine, dodging brooms,
Every daisy seems to giggle,
As we tend, we can't help but wiggle.

Roses blush with gossip shared,
Tulips cheer, we've never fared,
Through weeds of worry, we still play,
A bumpy row, but hey, hooray!

Blossoms in the Breeze

Petals flutter on the wind,
Whispering secrets, they rescind,
We chase them all, on silly feet,
In this game, we can't be beat.

Dandelions spread with cheer,
Wishes fly, our hearts in gear,
With each puff, we laugh so wide,
In this joy, we two collide.

The Color of Us

In a world so bright and loud,
Two mismatched socks gather a crowd.
With polka dots and stripes they play,
Creating joy in a silly way.

We dance in hues of neon dreams,
Sipping sunshine in rainbow streams.
Laughter paints the air around,
As we skip together on painted ground.

Unfolding Together

Like origami in a breeze,
We fold and flip, then do as we please.
Paper hearts on a paper plane,
Gliding high, avoiding the rain.

We're like mismatched puzzle pieces,
Laughing loud as the fun increases.
Every fold a giggle shared,
In this crazy art, we are paired.

Melodies of the Heart

With a kazoo and a clumsy beat,
We make tunes that can't be beat.
Silly songs that make us grin,
Letting the joyful madness begin.

In harmony, we sing off-key,
A chorus of chuckles, you and me.
Strumming laughter on a ukulele,
Our anthem's a joyful melee.

Luminous Paths

We wander trails of sparkly light,
Wearing mismatched shoes; what a sight!
Chasing giggles through a glittered haze,
Our footsteps dance in a silly daze.

With lanterns made of jelly beans,
Lighting paths like festive scenes.
We stroll hand-in-hand, side by side,
Creating laughter, our joyful guide.

The Embrace of Dreams

In the land where wishes sprout,
Naps are traded, no doubt.
Pillow fights with giggles abound,
Dreams are lost, then refound.

Jellybeans dance on a breeze,
Whispers tease like bumblebees.
Pickle jars that sing at night,
Dance with socks, oh what a sight!

Clouds wear hats of fluffy cream,
Catching stars, oh what a dream.
Giggles echo, bouncing high,
As laughter floats and swirls the sky.

Under sheets of twinkling gleam,
Close your eyes, let's make a team.
In this space, we twist and twirl,
Where fun sprouts, and laughter whirls!

Footsteps in the Sun

Sunny paths where shadows play,
Chasing toes, hippos say hooray.
Flip-flops flap like joyful birds,
As laughter spills with silly words.

Crispy fries on golden plates,
Tickle fights with twisty fates.
Ice cream drips and giggles flow,
In warm embrace, we steal the show.

Kites are dancing, flying high,
While clowns juggle, oh my, oh my!
Chase the clouds, they slip and slide,
Under the sun, we take a ride.

Banana peels and games galore,
Skipping stones, then rolling on the floor.
In the warmth, our hearts have spun,
Together, we blend, two becoming one!

Seeds of Affection

In a garden of giggles, we plant our dreams,
With love in our pockets and silly ice creams.
Watering with laughter, we dance in delight,
Grows a patch of kindness, all day and all night.

Daisies keep whispering, 'You're the best joke,'
While bees buzz around wearing hats, oh what a cloak!
We prune back the worry, give weeds a good laugh,
In this wild love patch, we're all on the path.

Blossoms of the Heart

Tickles from petals, as we stroll through the park,
A bouquet of giggles, it brightens the dark.
We plant our corny puns under sunshine's grin,
Watch the flowers blossom, let the fun begin!

With pollen of joy, we spread some pure glee,
As butterflies chuckle, chasing you and me.
We skip through the laughter, in this bloom of mirth,
Growing side by side, we're a laugh-filled girth.

Threads of Connection

Tangled in humor, our yarns intertwine,
Sewing socks of silliness, oh how divine!
Each stitch of affection, a giggle and grin,
Woven with warmth, let the fun times begin.

We knit up our moments, a blanket of cheer,
While friends bring confetti, with each silly leer.
Unravel the worries, let the joy flow free,
In this crazy tapestry, just you wait and see!

Nurtured Emotions

In a pot full of chuckles, we sow what we feel,
Watering with kindness, it's a wacky deal.
With sunshine of smirks and laughter so bright,
Our garden of giggles blooms every night.

Fertilized with kindness, it's a love of its own,
With herbs of humor, we've happily grown.
So let's dance through the daisies, don't stay in a frown,
In this nurtured laughter, wear your joy like a crown!

Embracing the Unseen

In a world of little surprises,
We sneak love like hidden pies.
With giggles tucked in each heart,
It's a joy, the best kind of art.

Invisible hugs in crowded rooms,
Spreading laughter like wild blooms.
We dance with shadows, chase the light,
And share our secrets out of sight.

A wink exchanged between old friends,
A joke that never really ends.
We paint the walls with silly dreams,
And laugh 'til nothing's as it seems.

In twilight's glow, our spirits twist,
A comedy we can't resist.
With every chuckle, bonds we grow,
In the silliness, true love will flow.

The Bouquet of Us

Picture flowers in a vase,
Each petal bright, a funny face.
We mix the colors, bold and neat,
Creating chaos that feels sweet.

With daisies dressed in silly hats,
We dance around like playful rats.
Sunflowers giggle, roses wink,
In our bouquet, joy's on the brink.

As bees buzz in their merry chase,
We share our quirks with each embrace.
Laughter wrapped in leafy greens,
Life's punchlines stitching up the seams.

So here we stand, a wacky crew,
Blooming wildly, just me and you.
In every giggle, love's scent swells,
A beautiful tale that laughter tells.

Tides of Togetherness

We ride the waves of humor's grace,
With splashes true, this lively space.
A surfboard made of giggling dreams,
   We navigate with silly schemes.

Waves of laughter crash the sand,
With every joke, we take a stand.
Seashell whispers join the fun,
With every smile, our hearts are one.

As tides swing back and forth in bliss,
We're caught in joy with every kiss.
A lighthouse shines, keeps our path clear,
   With cheeky grins and hearty cheer.

In ocean's arms, we float and sway,
   Embracing each ridiculous day.
Of tides and laughter, we're well aware,
   Together we rise, and then we share.

Harvesting Harmony

In fields of humor, we gather cheer,
With giggles ripe, the end is near.
We plant our seeds of wit and charm,
And watch them grow with endless balm.

Each crop a tale, each fruit a jest,
Life's funny moments put to the test.
We reap the laughter, sift the fun,
Under the warm, forgiving sun.

As veggies dance in wild delight,
We cook up love both day and night.
With every bite, a chuckle shared,
In every dish, our hearts are bared.

So let's toast to the wit we raise,
In silly harvests, we sing our praise.
With every belly laugh and cheer,
We sow the joy that draws us near.

Blossoms at Dusk

In gardens where the daisies dance,
A bee and the flower share a glance.
The sun winks, oh cheeky thing,
As petals blush, ready to spring.

A squirrel tries to steal a kiss,
From the wind that makes him miss.
Love blooms in the soft twilight,
With giggles echoing through the night.

Crickets croon their silly tunes,
While moonbeams match their funky moves.
The stars laugh in a glittering spree,
As nature plays comedy so free.

While the daisies dream of romps and fun,
Every evening sets the mood for one.
With whispers sweet and laughter loud,
Blossoms dance, they're simply proud!

Love Like Light

Through beams that stretch across the sky,
A toaster pops; it's breakfast time, oh my!
The butter melts with a sizzle and gleam,
Like two hearts caught in a dream.

A lightbulb flickers overhead,
It winks at the jam, 'Let's spread!'
Toast and honey hold a meeting,
To discuss the warmth they're beating.

Laughter dances in the kitchen's air,
As pancake flips land here and there.
The coffee brews with comic flair,
In love's aroma, giggles share.

In this place where bright thoughts spark,
Each morning's glow ignites the dark.
With every drip, a sweet delight,
Every chuckle, love feels right.

Mosaic of Emotions

With crayons strewn across the floor,
A masterpiece of laughter galore.
Each stroke a giggle, each color a cheer,
Crafting memories we hold dear.

The green is for the jellybeans shared,
Blue represents how much we cared.
Red splatters tell of silly fights,
And yellow shines on our happy nights.

Glue sticks stick but they don't know,
How friendship grows with every row.
As we doodle dreams, create and play,
In this canvas, love finds its way.

As thoughts collide and wild colors blend,
We create a puzzle with no end.
In our silly art, emotions unfurl,
A mosaic of joy in a colorful swirl.

The Unfolding Journey

With each step on this winding path,
We step in puddles without any wrath.
The sun peeks out, then hides away,
As laughter chases clouds astray.

In the line for ice cream, we giggle and sway,
As flavors swirl in a happy display.
With sprinkles on top, we take a bite,
A sugary treat to spark delight.

Each twist and turn, a new surprise,
Like shoelaces tied in clever disguise.
We tumble and roll, but with a grin,
In our playful race, love starts to win.

Through ups and downs, we dance and fall,
The journey is sweet; it's the best of all.
With every tick of the clock, we learn,
In this merry chase, it's love we earn.

Sweet Serenade of Togetherness

In a garden of giggles, we play,
Planting dreams in a comical way.
With heart-shaped seeds, we throw and toss,
Giggling together, we'll never be lost.

Watering smiles with ice cream delight,
In this patch of joy, everything feels right.
We dance with bees in our silly routine,
Two goofy hearts in a love-themed scene.

Each flower we plant has a funny face,
To bloom in a world filled with warmth and grace.
With puns in the petals and laugh in the air,
Together we blossom, without a care.

So here's to our journey, both silly and sweet,
In this love garden, where laughter's the treat.
With each little bud, let our humor grow,
In this serenade, we put on a show.

Shimmering Threads

We weave our days with bright, silly yarn,
Stitching laughter, our hearts go on a charm.
With needles of joy, we poke and prod,
Creating a quilt, not a single facade.

Tangled in giggles, we thread our fate,
Bobbing like clowns, on a love merry-go-rate.
Each patch tells a joke that's slightly absurd,
In this wacky fabric, our hearts are stirred.

Sewing up smiles with a dash of delight,
In a cozy embrace, everything feels right.
We snip out the worries, and sew in the cheer,
With every loop spun, love's whisper is clear.

So here's to our tapestry, so bright and bold,
Made of laughter and stories yet to be told.
Each shimmering thread a sweet little quirk,
In our patchwork of joy, we go on berserk.

The Sweetness We Cultivate

In the garden of giggles, we plant our dreams,
Watering with jokes, laughter bursts at the seams.
With a sprinkle of puns and a dollop of cheer,
Cultivating sweetness year after year.

Each silly sprout has a story to tell,
Growing together, we giggle and yell.
Plot twists of joy in this quirky terrain,
In our patch of delight, there's never a strain.

We pluck ripe memories with whimsical glee,
Savoring the flavors of all we can be.
In this playful field, where happiness calls,
We gather the giggles that dance through our halls.

So come join this harvest, as laughter we reap,
In the sweetness we gather, our hearts take a leap.
With each chuckle and snicker, our joy is true,
In this garden of whimsy, there's always room for two.

Hidden Blooms of Affection

Among the weeds, we find our delight,
Hidden blooms of affection, the silliest sight.
With quirky petals shaped like our grins,
In this wild patchwork, love always wins.

Beneath the dirt, we giggle and play,
Each flower's a joke that brightens our day.
With roots intertwined in a crazy embrace,
Our hearts are the sunlight in this funny space.

As we dig up the laughter, what treasures we find,
A bouquet of chuckles, so whimsically combined.
In this hidden garden, where joy takes its stand,
We spread blossoms of giggles across the land.

So let's wander the aisles of our aww-inspiring spree,
Finding blooms of affection, just you and me.
In this riot of colors, we bloom ever bright,
Love's hidden treasures, a comical sight.

Beneath the Surface

In the quiet corners, hearts do giggle,
Underneath laughter, they wiggle and wiggle.
A wink here, a nudge there, so sly and sweet,
Like two left feet on a dance floor fleet.

Whispers of antics, like ducks in a row,
With a splash of humor, they steal the show.
Just look at those two, under the moonlight,
Cracking up jokes, till dawn comes in sight.

Beneath all the banter, a secret does bloom,
Sprouting hilarity in every room.
Silly little moments, in each other's dish,
Who knew hearts could work with a giggly swish?

So here's to the chuckles, the jests that they share,
Pouring out love, like confetti in air.
With glances so playful and smiles so bright,
They'll dance through the day, into the night!

Love's Gentle Revolution

In a world spinning round, it's a comical fight,
With hearts in the ring, they reel left and right.
A soft touch, a tickle, mixed in with glee,
They plot silly schemes, just like a movie spree.

Cupid's been busy, with bows made of cheese,
Hurling his arrows, aiming to please.
He trips and he fumbles, what a sight to behold,
Each love-struck moment just never gets old.

Balancing laughter on a tightrope of fate,
Those heartbeats march on, in a funny gait.
With banners of jesting, they march into spring,
While singing off-key, oh, what joy they bring!

Revolution's a romp, with sparkles and cheer,
Each tickle and snort brings the dear ones near.
So gather your giggles, let the good times unfold,
A comedy of love, the best tale ever told!

The Dance of Hearts

With jazz hands waving, hearts take to the floor,
Twisting and turning, they crave for more.
Each stir of laughter is a step that they take,
In this grand illusion, there's no way to fake.

Balloons are their partners, as pie in the sky,
They trip over kittens, oh my, oh my!
A jolly old tango that makes them all grin,
Spilling sweet jokes, like confetti within.

Two clumsy souls in a rhythm divine,
Frolicking wildly, is it love? No, it's a line!
With two left feet on a slick dance floor,
It's all just a wiggle, who could ask for more?

With each twirl and twizzle, a giggle erupts,
As the crowd of affection eagerly erupts.
So grab your partner, sway with delight,
For the dance of the heart is a marvelous sight!

The Language of Embrace

In the arms of a friend, they laugh loud and free,
Silly stories bubble like sweet cups of tea.
A hug full of giggles, a squeeze that's a shove,
The secret's in jest, with a twist of the glove.

Whispers of mischief, as serious as pie,
With hugs that are stickers, potential to fly.
A belly laugh buried in a warm, sweet squeeze,
Making room for joy, like a fun summer breeze.

Their smiles conversation, no words need to thread,
Just crinkled up eyes, and the joy they spread.
A poke for affection, a nudge for a grin,
The beauty of closeness, where laughter begins.

So gather around, for a hug that's divine,
With tickles and gaffes in the grand design.
In this quirky embrace, love takes its place,
With humor the language, they all gladly chase!

Blossoming Embrace

In a garden of giggles, we plant silly seeds,
Sunshine and laughter fulfill all our needs.
With every chuckle, a flower will grow,
Watch as the petals of friendship do glow.

Planting our hopes with a wink and a grin,
We'll dance with the daisies, let the fun begin.
Roses are red, but the jokes are a blast,
Growing a patch where good vibes are cast.

Chasing the bees, wearing hats quite sublime,
Sipping on smoothies, enjoying the rhyme.
Whenever we stumble, we burst out in cheer,
Our love's like a party, a joy-filled frontier.

So here's to our blooms, both silly and bright,
In this garden of humor, we find pure delight.
Together we flourish, with puns that uplift,
In this blossoming tale, we share the best gift.

Heartstrings Entwined

With shoelaces tangled, we run side by side,
Our hearts do the limbo, let laughter be our guide.
In every mix-up, we find something sweet,
Like two goofy confections, we're quite the treat.

When you trip over smiles, don't worry, it's cool,
We'll giggle together, it's our special rule.
Tugging on heartstrings, we play like a band,
Creating a melody, hand in hand.

Whiskered cats playing with yarn so divine,
Our friendship's a dance—awkward yet fine.
With every misstep, we skip and we sway,
In this joyful ballet, come join in the play.

So let's tie our hearts in a comical knot,
With puns and confetti, we'll give it a shot.
In the symphony of giggles, we shall perfectly blend,
Two hearts in a twist, forever friends at the end.

Nurtured Connections

We sprout like radishes, oh so quirky and bold,
In our garden of giggles, friendship's pure gold.
We water with puns and sprinkle some cheer,
Nurturing connections with laughter so dear.

With high-fives like sunshine, we brighten the day,
In this patch of delight, we frolic and play.
Planting our dreams with a dash of delight,
Our hearts like young sprouts reach for the light.

When troubles arise, we'll just giggle and shrug,
Bouncing like bunnies, or perhaps like a bug.
In tangled-up roots, where our laughter does dwell,
Nurtured connections make a magical spell.

So here's to our garden, where silliness reigns,
With friendship's fresh soil, we dance in the rains.
Together we flourish, planting seeds of the heart,
In this whimsical realm, we'll never drift apart.

Echoes of Kindness

Shouting out kindness to every nearby ear,
We echo our laughter, spreading joy without fear.
In this carnival ride, we twist and we twirl,
Creating a whirlwind, oh what a fun swirl!

Tickles of humor bounce off every wall,
We're like two balloons, having the time of our fall.
With each silly jest, we toss kindness like confetti,
Building a fortress where hearts feel all-ready.

When the world seems so grumpy, we dance in the rain,
Spreading our cheer like a sweet candy cane.
In echoes of kindness, we find our true sound,
Two comical souls in a world quite profound.

So let's make some memories, silly and bright,
With laughter as fuel, we'll take off in flight.
In this joyful cacophony, our hearts will align,
In the echoes of goodness, we'll forever shine.

A Symphony of Souls

In the dance of a clumsy pair,
Two hearts tripped over the air.
He spilled his drink, she let out a snort,
Their laughter echoed, a joyful sort.

They tried to share a single fry,
But one got snagged, oh my, oh my!
With every nibble, giggles increased,
In sauce and mirth, their hearts were released.

A serenade of snorts and sighs,
Who knew romance could come in such guise?
With every blunder and silly face,
They found their rhythm, a timeless embrace.

As mismatched socks dance on the floor,
Their quirky love sprouted evermore.
In silly chaos, bonds reside,
A symphony of souls in a joyful ride.

Radiant Bonds

In a race to the fridge, she slipped, oh dear,
His laughter rang out, music to hear.
They bumped together, a glorious crash,
As snacks exploded in a hilarious splash.

With popcorn scattered like stars in the night,
They both stretched to grab it; what a sight!
His hand met hers in a buttery mess,
They stood laughing, their hearts in excess.

A tickle fight broke out, feathers flew,
In the middle of mess, love in view.
Each giggle echoed in their little space,
Creating a bond with a humorous grace.

Their quirks like constellations aligned,
In their zany world, the stars brightly shined.
With every mishap, a chance to grow,
Radiant bonds in the laughter's glow.

Tender Moments in Time

On a park bench, they shared a pie,
One bite at a time as the birds flew by.
But pie got smashed and whipped cream flew,
A frothy battle, love in the brew.

With sticky fingers and frosting smiles,
They mapped out dreams, danced with guiles.
Each moment tender, wrapped in delight,
As squirrels cheered on their obvious plight.

She said, "You're my favorite weirdo, you see,"
He grinned back and said, "Right back at me!"
In the glow of the sun and a sprinkle of fun,
They unearthed a love that had only begun.

In laughter's embrace, they learned to climb,
Collecting sweet memories, one whimsical rhyme.
Like clouds that giggle, each day truly shines,
Tender moments, perfect as fine-woven twines.

Love's Gentle Evolution

From awkward glances to giggles loud,
Two minds hilariously joined the crowd.
With each small blunder, sparks they did find,
As paths twisted softly, blissfully entwined.

Like puppies at play, chasing their tails,
Their lives morphed into joyful trails.
Every misstep a lesson in dance,
With each silly moment, they took a chance.

From cereal spills to mismatched socks,
Their laughter rang out; it never blocks.
Through moments giddy, their hearts revised,
In love's gentle evolution, humor's the prize.

With every joke, a layer unfurled,
As they strolled hand in hand through this whimsical world.
Armed with laughter, they co-wrote their fate,
In joyful absurdity, they'd celebrate.

Fragrance of Unity

In a world of giggles and grins,
Laughter sprinkles like cinnamon spins.
We share our snacks, we toast our bread,
In each silly moment, love's easily fed.

Tickling fancies, like cats in a chase,
Clumsy heart dances, a wild, funny race.
We plant seeds of joy in our quirky way,
Sprouting smiles in the silliest play.

Jellybean rainbows in mismatched shoes,
Spilling joy like colorful hues.
Every chuckle, a blossom anew,
Our hearts bloom bright, like flowers in dew.

So let's giggle and romp, never grow old,
In this garden of jest, our stories unfold.
For in laughter's embrace, we find our light,
A fragrance of unity, sweet and bright.

The Dance of Hearts

Two left feet in a shuffle so grand,
We whirl and twirl, a comical band.
With mismatched moves, we stumble and sway,
In every misstep, we're dancing away.

Add a sprinkle of laughter, a dash of cheer,
Our hearts beat together, the rhythm is clear.
We laugh at the timing, so wonderfully wrong,
Yet somehow, our dance feels like a love song.

Funky steps lead us to unexpected places,
With giggles that echo, and silly faces.
A tango of tickles, a waltz of delight,
When we join hands, the world feels light.

So let's dance through the chaos, not footloose and free,
With chuckles that gather like confetti from me.
In this funny ballet, forever we'll dart,
Creating a symphony, a dance of the heart.

A Tangle of Emotions

Like yarn in a cat's playful embrace,
Our feelings are tangled, a comical chase.
Each twist and each knot, silly stories unite,
In the mess of our hearts, the laughter ignites.

One day it's joy, the next it's a pout,
Riding the rollercoaster, with shouts and a sprout.
We're puzzles of giggles, wherever we go,
A tapestry woven with love's goofy flow.

Like spaghetti spilled under the moon,
Our emotions dance to a whimsical tune.
In the chaos, we find what makes us feel bright,
A tangle of warmth in the soft, starlit night.

So embrace every mix-up, every hijinks spree,
For tangled emotions just mean we're so free.
In this quirky mess lies the charm of our art,
Binding us closer, each laugh from the heart.

Cherished Echoes

The echoes of laughter bounce off the wall,
In this whimsical space, we're having a ball.
Like echoes of giggles that linger and play,
In the cherished moments, we brighten the day.

"Did you trip or was it a dance?" we snicker,
Finding joy in the fall, love grows even quicker.
Every punchline shared, a spark in the night,
In the heart's echo chamber, everything feels right.

We share cherished tales over cups of hot tea,
With each silly story, we twist and we tee.
Two peas in a pod or a pair of old shoes,
In this laughter echo, there's nothing to lose.

So come join the chorus of hearts all around,
In this whimsical journey, pure joy will abound.
With echoes of love, our laughter flows free,
In every chuckle we share, you'll find me.

Cultivating Warmth

In the garden of giggles, we plant a joke,
With water from laughter, and light from a poke.
Sprinkle some kindness, toss in a pun,
Watch it all blossom, oh what fun!

Compost your worries, let chuckles grow,
Weaving silliness in every row.
Prune away frowns, let joy take the lead,
And fertilize smiles with a kind word seed.

Dance with the daisies, tickle the breeze,
A patchwork of chuckles, oh if you please!
In this field of friendship, let quirks unite,
We'll harvest affection, all day and night.

So grab your spade and dig with glee,
Plant a joke here, and a giggle tree.
With laughter and warmth, we'll make it, you see,
A garden of joy, just you and me.

The Growth of Tenderness

With a sprinkle of chaos and a dash of cheer,
We water the roots of the ones we hold dear.
A seed of a hug, a handful of care,
Watch as connections begin to flare.

In a pot full of quirks, let our weirdness thrive,
We'll nurture and feather the dreams come alive.
A mix of oddities, all in one place,
Cultivating kindness with every embrace.

Harvest the giggles from shared silly tales,
Sow moments that shimmer like soft morning gales.
We'll prune out the grumps and let joy take flight,
Growing tenderness, so sweetly bright.

So come plant your heart in this whimsical plot,
Let's dance in the sunlight, give it all that we've got.
In this jolly garden, forever abide,
With a smile on our faces, and love as our guide.

Whispers of Devotion

In the midnight garden where shadows play,
We whisper sweet secrets in a silly way.
A tickle from petals, a wink from the moon,
Our laughter echoes, like a funny tune.

With mischief and mayhem, we plant our roots,
Building bonds stronger than old, worn-out boots.
Each giggle a promise, each chuckle a sign,
In this plot of affection, our spirits entwine.

We'll nurture our dreams with a sprinkle of spice,
Toss in some humor, isn't that nice?
In the whispers of night, let our hearts convene,
Creating a symphony, silly and serene.

So let's sow our giggles, let's cultivate fun,
With devotion a-plenty, we've only begun.
In the garden of joy where affection takes flight,
Let's dance under starlight, glowing so bright.

Sowing Sweetness

Gather round, friends, it's planting time,
With sprinkles of sugar and a hint of rhyme.
We'll toss in some giggles, let kindness sprout,
In the soil of friendship, there's never a doubt.

From cupcakes to candor, we plant with flair,
A dash of delight, oh, we've got to share!
We'll water with joy and prune all the gloom,
Watching our laughter reach full bloom.

Each little seedling, a story to tell,
Flavors of sweetness, oh can you smell?
In the orchard of silly, let love unfold,
Harvesting moments worth more than gold.

So grab your trowel, let's dig in the fun,
Sow a patch of sweetness, for everyone!
In this wonderful garden, together we'll grow,
With hearts intertwined, let affection overflow.

The Light We Share

In a world full of giggles, we spread joy,
Like kids with a new shiny toy.
With hearts that balloon like bubbles in air,
We shine out our laughter, a luminous flare.

Jokes that are silly, puns that just fly,
Our smiles are contagious; don't even ask why.
With every snicker, we light up the night,
Together we sparkle, a comical sight.

Winds of Affection

In the breezy whispers, we blow each kiss,
Like dandelion seeds dancing in bliss.
Our hearts are kites strung on colorful strings,
Floating on laughter, oh the joy that it brings!

With every gust, we send out a cheer,
Silly winds of fondness, can you hear?
We twirl in the zephyrs, love's jest in the air,
As we skip through the meadows without a care.

Stars in Our Eyes

With twinkling glances, we share the skies,
Like popcorn in buckets, laughter never lies.
Under moonlight, we sparkle and gleam,
In this funny universe, we're a wild dream.

We trade comets for giggles, laugh until sore,
Creating constellations in joy we explore.
With each blissful chuckle, a galaxy grows,
Love and humor in orbit, everybody knows.

Gathering Embrace

In a circle of hugs, we welcome the fun,
Like a pot of warm soup shared by everyone.
With tickles and whispers, we gather near,
A melting pot of joy, with laughter we cheer.

Tangled in silliness, we create a mess,
Knotty bundles of fun, love's sweet caress.
As we bounce in our hugs like soft marshmallow,
Together we giggle, and the world feels mellow.

The Blooming Spirit

In a garden where jokes take flight,
Flowers bloom with pure delight.
Bees giggle as they hum along,
Wearing tiny hats—they can't go wrong!

Sunflowers wink at the morning dew,
Roses blush at a sky so blue.
Laughter sprouts from every petal,
As daisies dance on the garden metal.

Gardens chat in the evening glow,
Telling secrets that only they know.
With every chuckle, the colors blend,
Painting a scene that will never end.

Kindling the Fire Within

A spark ignites, like silly sparks,
Tickling toes while chasing larks.
The flames of joy dance wild and free,
Making marshmallows sing with glee!

Gather 'round, bring your best jokes,
We kindle warmth as laughter pokes.
Roasting dreams on a stick of fun,
Each smile lighting up the run!

Even shadows chuckle and sway,
As embers bounce in a cheeky play.
In this fiery furnace of delight,
We all glow brightly, day and night!

Harvesting Sweetness

In the fields of giggles, we collect,
Berries of laughter we can't neglect.
Grapes of joy stomped beneath our feet,
Juice of happiness, oh so sweet!

We plant our seeds with a wink and a grin,
Water them daily with a chuckle or spin.
The crops grow tall, with roots deep in cheer,
Harvesting sweetness all through the year!

Baskets full of joy load up the truck,
As friends join in, they bring their luck.
We share the feast, but still capture the fun,
In the festival of laughter, we are all one!

The Language of Emotions

With a flick and a giggle, we speak our heart,
In a dialect of joy, a true work of art.
A wink can convey what words cannot say,
A silly dance can brighten the gray.

With high-fives and chuckles, we build a bridge,
Connecting our feelings like a fun ridge.
Every smile a sentence; laughter the key,
Opening doors to our hearts, you see!

Emotions tumble like marbles in play,
Each one colored in a quirky way.
So let's laugh together, with zest and with cheer,
In this silly language, there's nothing to fear!

Petals of Understanding

In a garden where feelings bloom,
We giggle with petals, there's plenty of room.
With watering can, we'll both take a shot,
Just don't pour too heavy, or watch for the spot.

We pluck silly daisies, our secrets they trace,
With laughter and mischief, we dance in this space.
Each petal a story, we share with delight,
Creating a bouquet that sparkles so bright.

Chasing the bees, oh what a wild chase,
Buzzing and teasing, we brighten the place.
With a wink and a nod, we tie up our hearts,
Crafting a wonder that never departs.

So if you see blooms, know they've got flair,
They whisper our secrets through sweet summer air.
In this garden of humor, we plant our delight,
With petals of understanding, everything's bright.

Rooted In Us

We plant our jokes deep, like roots in the ground,
Each punchline a sprout, with laughter unbound.
Tangled and twisted, our humor takes hold,
Through snickers and snorts, our stories unfold.

With shovels of kindness, we dig and we delve,
Creating a forest of fun, just ourselves.
Branches that sway in the funniest breeze,
We'll tickle the soil, put the world at ease.

Growing together, our quirks intertwine,
In this garden of goofiness, everything's fine.
We water with smiles, our roots run so deep,
Through laughter, our love is the harvest we reap.

So let's plant a tree, let's watch it all grow,
With branches of joy in a comedy show.
Rooted in us, we're a riot, it's true,
Forever entwined, just me and you.

Compassionate Currents

Riding the waves of a giggly tide,
With kindness and chuckles, together we glide.
Splashing in humor, oh what a sight,
We twirl in the current from morning till night.

In puddles of laughter, our worries float by,
With rubber duck dreams, we aim for the sky.
Beneath rainbow waters, our hearts feel so free,
Just don't rock the boat; it's funnier, you see?

We surf through set-backs, let's wipe out with glee,
Our friendship's the ocean; there's room for a spree.
With waves of compassion, we paddle along,
In this quirky sea, we know we belong.

So dive in with giggles, feel the splash where you are,
In this sea of delight, we'll be your guiding star.
Compassionate currents will take us afar,
Just don't ask the fish how we got this bizarre!

Fields of Care

In fields of green giggles, we scatter our cheer,
With windmills of kindness, we'll spin, persevere.
Tickling the daisies with laughter so bright,
We'll frolic together till day turns to night.

With baskets of jokes and hugs in our nets,
We'll gather up moments, no regrets, no debts.
We dance through the daisies, twirling around,
Finding joy in each step as we leap from the ground.

Come join this fair party, let's skip without fear,
With socks full of sunshine, we'll spread joy right here.
In this field of care, we plant seeds of delight,
Growing hearts like flowers, all blooming just right.

So prance with abandon, let's make some new rules,
In the fields of our friendship, we're both just like fools.
With love in the air and a wink in our stare,
We'll cultivate happiness, it's truly quite rare!

Ripples of Affection

In a pond where ducks do quack,
A heart sends waves, no looking back.
The frogs join in, they do a dance,
While fish shake fins in a romance.

Sprinkling smiles, the breeze takes flight,
As shy clouds giggle, feeling light.
With every splash, we laugh and sing,
Creating joy, it's a silly thing.

Together, We Grow

Two little seeds in a garden bed,
Wiggled their roots, and shared some bread.
With whispers soft, they shared their dreams,
Of flowers bright and sunlit beams.

The worms join in, with jokes to share,
As raindrops fall, they dance in air.
Though one is tall and one is small,
Together they bloom, they stand up tall.

The Light We Share

A candle flickers on a noodle plate,
While spaghetti twirls, they flirt with fate.
As garlic bread gives a hearty cheer,
The kitchen hums; love is near!

In toasty warmth, the shadows play,
They whisper secrets, night turns to day.
With giggles bright, they light the way,
A feast of laughs, together they stay.

Love's Underground Roots

Beneath the soil, a party stirs,
With moles and bugs, and dancing furs.
They tell the tales of love's sweet song,
While sneaky roots just sing along.

In tunnels deep, they laugh out loud,
Creating bonds that feel so proud.
Each little laugh gives life a tug,
As nature sways, in a big old hug.

A Garden of Kindness

In a garden of smiles, we plant our seeds,
Watered with laughter, sprouting good deeds.
Each hug's a petal, each joke a sunbeam,
Together we flourish, like a wild, wacky dream.

Bees buzz with glee, spreading joy all around,
In this quirky patch, silliness abounds.
Whimsy in rows, with a sprinkle of cheer,
Tickles and giggles, that's how we steer!

Sunflowers dancing, in the breeze they sway,
Chasing the clouds, and the grumps away.
With each silly story, we water our crop,
In this garden of giggles, we never stop!

So join the fun folks, in this patch of good cheer,
Bring your odd jokes, and a pinch of weird.
For love is a riddle, a raucous delight,
In the garden of kindness, everything's bright!

Echoes of Amity

In the hall of echoes, friendships abound,
With laughter that bounces, a sweet, silly sound.
Tossing out puns, like confetti in air,
Let's tickle the echoes, without a care!

Whispers of kindness, in each corner they play,
Skip through the shadows, and dance in the day.
With a wink and a smile, we share our delight,
In the world of amity, we shine so bright!

Jokes weave the tales, like ribbons so fine,
Creating connections that twinkle and twine.
So grab a good friend, and let's make a scene,
In the echoes of laughter, we're comfy and keen!

Let's chase the giggles, and never look back,
For echoes of joy keep our hearts on track.
In this silly assembly, we gather and cheer,
With laughter as our tune, we have nothing to fear!

Watering the Spirit

With a sprinkle of joy, we douse our days,
Pouring kindness like water, in the sun's warm rays.
Silly dreams blossom, in pots full of cheer,
Let's water the spirit, let's laugh without fear!

A splash of chortles, a dash of delight,
In this garden of giggles, everything's bright.
We're gardeners of whimsy, you know it's true,
Tending to memories, with a giggling crew!

So grab your watering can, let's shower the love,
With each hearty laugh, we rise like a dove.
Our spirits are blooming, bursting with zest,
In this garden of humor, we're truly blessed!

Let's grow our connections, with quips and with glee,
Nurturing wonders, together you and me.
With every chuckle, we brighten the space,
Watering the spirit, a dear, funny place!

Flourishing Bonds

Bonds grow like wildflowers, sprouting each day,
Sowed in the soil of fun, come what may.
With every goofy story, we plant our roots,
Growing together, in our comical suits!

Twisting and turning, our laughter entwined,
In this garden of friendship, hilarity's blind.
Trellises holding, our quirks on display,
In the sunshine of joy, we'll forever stay!

So let's twirl together in a wacky parade,
Hand in hand giggling; no debts to be paid.
Our laughter's the music, a joyful ballet,
In the flourishing bonds, come join the play!

With hearts intertwined, we'll tackle the day,
In this whimsical patch, we'll frolic and sway.
For bonds that are strong, can weather the storm,
And in the laughter of bonds, we feel so warm!

Serene Connections

In a garden where laughter grows,
The plants giggle, everyone knows.
Sunflowers wink at the bees in flight,
While daisies dance in pure delight.

With gnomes who tell silly tales,
And butterflies donning tiny veils,
They sip on nectar with flair and glee,
Sharing secrets as sweet as can be.

The breeze tickles the leaves so bright,
As ladybugs twirl out of sheer delight.
In this patch, love's a playful game,
Where every bloom thinks they're a fame.

When raindrops fall, they splash and play,
Creating puddles for friends to sway.
In this funny, vibrant garden bright,
Connections bloom, oh what a sight!

Beyond the Horizon

Up on the hill where the sky meets the sea,
Laughter floats up like a kite set free.
Clouds wear hats, and the sun grins wide,
While waves play tag, rolling in with pride.

Sailing boats with silly names,
Guffawing at their own little games.
Seagulls squawking jokes in the air,
While crabs boogie down without a care.

At twilight, colors blend and swirl,
Whispering secrets to the next twirl.
The horizon winks, a glimmering tease,
Holding connections like falling leaves.

In this quirky place, love's a play,
Where every moment's an irony ballet.
Beyond the horizon, hearts gleam and beam,
In a world where humor reigns supreme.

Whispers of the Heart

Little birds chirp silly tunes,
Underneath the broad light of the moon.
Even the owls hoot in a groove,
As night plays its mischievous move.

A squirrel tells jokes in a tree,
To a rabbit who hops with glee.
Raccoons roll about, oh what a sight,
As stars giggle in the soft moonlight.

Petals whisper secrets so sweet,
As caterpillars tap their tiny feet.
In the crazy world of the night,
Every shadow shares love at first sight.

With each rustle, hearts unite,
In this wondrous and whimsical night.
Nature's laughter, a joyful part,
Whispering softly, the song of the heart.

Seeds of Affection

In the sandbox where friendships bloom,
We plant our dreams with fun, not gloom.
With shovels and buckets, we dig away,
Creating castles where we love to play.

A sprinkle of giggles, a dash of cheers,
Building our towers, conquering fears.
Marshmallow clouds float up so high,
As kites dance above in the open sky.

The sun winks down, pretending to tease,
While sand crabs dance in the playful breeze.
Every grain tells a joke, a hearty roar,
As whispers of joy settle to the floor.

In this garden of play, love doth grow,
With raucous laughter and treats in tow.
So here we stay, adorned in delight,
In the seeds of affection, our hearts take flight.

Radiance of Togetherness

In a world where socks disappear,
We find joy in shared pizza, oh dear!
Laughing at memes, in pajamas we lay,
Creating our chaos, in a joyful ballet.

With mismatched shoes and hair that's a mess,
We dance like no one cares about our stress.
Sprinkling kindness like we sprinkle cheese,
Well, even in quirks, they never fail to please.

Walking on sunshine, we wear silly hats,
Trading old stories with giggles and spats.
Our hearts beam brightly, like disco balls spin,
Together we're stronger, let the fun begin!

With ice cream mountains, we're sticky and sweet,
Every shared smile is a silly treat.
In laughter we gather, our friendship's so bright,
Together we shine, like stars in the night.

A Palette of Affection

We paint our days with bursts of fun,
In a canvas of chaos, we have just begun.
With splashes of laughter and drips of delight,
Our masterpiece sparkles, oh what a sight!

Like colors that mix, we're vibrant and free,
Creating a whirlwind of harmony.
Using crayons of kindness, we doodle and play,
In a world full of chuckles, we'll brighten the day.

Every mishap's a giggle, each slip's a new song,
In our silly duet, there's nothing wrong.
As we splash through puddles and bask in the sun,
We treasure these moments, they're so much fun!

So come join our palette, let's paint it with cheer,
With hues of affection, our bonds are sincere.
In this gallery of friendship, our laughter won't stop,
Together we rise, and together we hop!

The Glow of Kinship

In this bright little bubble, we laugh till we cry,
With pretzel hugs and truths that never lie.
Under the disco ball, we dance with glee,
Creating bright memories, just you and me.

With goofy grins and inside jokes shared,
In a tapestry of moments, we are prepared.
Chasing light beams with a burst of a giggle,
In the glow of our bond, we all dance and wiggle.

Through tickles and pranks, we keep it alive,
In the garden of friendship, we joyously thrive.
Hand in hand, we'll stroll, like a pair of clowns,
With laughter as currency, we'll never feel down.

So here's to the warmth that forever ignites,
In this glow of kinship, we reach new heights.
Let's keep the fire burning, through tickles and cheer,
With you by my side, every day's sunny here!

Weaving Warmth

In the quilt of our laughter, we stitch and we sew,
With threads of good humor, our feelings will grow.
Each patch tells a story, entwined with delight,
In the warmth of our hearts, we shine oh so bright.

We tangle like yarn in a playful embrace,
With retellings of blunders, we fill up the space.
Through ups and downs, our colors fuse well,
In the fabric of friendship, there's magic to tell.

With mismatched socks and cups filled with tea,
We brew up our joy quite hilariously.
As we knit up our dreams on this fun-loving loom,
Each weave is a chuckle, dispelling all gloom.

So let us gather closely, in this cozy nest,
Where laughter and love always manifest.
With stitches of kindness, our hearts will entwine,
In the warmth of togetherness, let us always shine!

Affectionate Footprints

Tiny shoes left by the door,
Pitter-patter, we want more!
Chasing giggles in the sand,
Hand in hand, it's quite grand.

Sometimes we trip, it's all good fun,
Laughter echoes, we run and run.
Heart-shaped cookies on a plate,
Sweet surprises, isn't love great?

Jumping over puddles with glee,
Splashing rainbows, just you and me.
Balloon animals float on by,
We chase them down, oh my, oh my!

With footprints scattered on the floor,
Each goofy dance opens a door.
Carefree moments, silly and bright,
Together we shine, a comical sight.

Treasures of the Heart

In a box of mismatched socks,
Lies the key to joy that unlocks.
Paper notes with doodles inside,
Treasuring moments we can't hide.

A rubber band ball gains some weight,
As we amass, it's quite the fate.
Chocolate wrappers spread about,
In this treasure, there's no doubt!

Laughter echoes in the kitchen,
Burnt toast made, oh it's glitchin'.
Whisking dreams like perfect eggs,
Silly laughter, joy unbegged.

Our little secrets, catapulted wide,
Treasure chests are where we bide.
With every giggle, our fortune grows,
In this wonder, our love glows.

Intertwined Destinies

Two straws twisted in a drink,
Sipping laughter, don't you think?
Pasta noodles, slurped with zeal,
Messy bites, that's the deal!

Matching socks, but one's a ghost,
Finding pairs is what we boast.
In our dance of twisted fate,
We find the joy while being late!

Pizza parties with silly hats,
Our pizza toppings have no spats.
Intertwined like vine and tree,
Branching out, how fun can we be?

Chasing dreams on our broken bikes,
Pedaling fast, love takes hikes.
With every tumble, every cheer,
We mark our path, both far and near.

The Canvas of Us

Splashes of colors in a mess,
Artistry born from our distress.
Each stroke giggles, a quirky line,
Creating moments that sparkle and shine.

Brushes dip in our laughter pot,
Painting pixels that we forgot.
Beet juice stains and glitter spills,
In this chaos, love just thrills!

Our masterpiece starts to bloom,
In a room filled with joyful gloom.
Clouds of cheese puffs on the floor,
Evidence of happiness galore.

When colors blend, it's a delight,
Every bump makes it feel just right.
On this canvas, we sketch our tale,
With giggles and splashes, we will not fail.

Flourishing Together

In the garden of hugs, we plant our seeds,
Watering laughter, pulling out weeds.
With sunshine smiles, we make them grow,
Two peas in a pod, just so you know.

We dance with the daisies, we twirl with glee,
Counting our blessings, just you and me.
We'd even hug thorns, for a joy-filled chase,
Blooming together, in this silly race.

Under moonlight's glow, we'll share our treats,
Chocolate and giggles, our favorite sweets.
With every silly joke that we both share,
Our colorful patch, beyond compare.

So grab that watering can, let's splash away,
In our vibrant garden, come what may.
Like sunflowers smiling, faces hold tight,
Flourishing together, what a delight!

The Dance of Devotion

With mismatched socks, we take the floor,
Grooving to rhythms, forevermore.
Twisting and turning, we trip and fall,
Laughter erupts, the best dance of all.

In our grand ballroom, the kitchen's a mess,
Flour on our noses, what a dress!
We shuffle and slide, and then do the crab,
With moves so silly, it drives us mad.

We twirl with passion, a spaghetti embrace,
No need for mirrors, just feel the space.
Chasing old socks around the room,
In this zany love, we always bloom.

So join the odd waltz, let nothing constrain,
Through every mishap, our joy won't wane.
The dance of devotion, stepped in delight,
We'll twirl through the chaos, hearts soaring high!

Sunlit Silhouettes

In the park's glow, we make shadow pets,
Squirrels and friends, no need for regrets.
Playing hopscotch on laughter's bright thread,
Mapping the dreams from our silly head.

With funky sunglasses and ice cream delight,
We chase down the sun, making sure it's bright.
Every giggle echoes through fragrant trees,
A symphony sung by the buzzing bees.

We cartwheel through puddles, no raincoat's a fuss,
With splashes and giggles, we create a plus.
Building dreams made of cotton candy fluff,
Life's a big joke, but we've got enough.

So let's create shadows, our own little show,
In this swirling dance, wherever we go.
Sunlit silhouettes, bright laughter anew,
Two jolly hearts, forever sticking like glue!

Heartfelt Horizon

At the edge of the day, we build sandy towers,
Talking to crabs, sharing our powers.
With seashells as crowns, we're rulers of fun,
Chasing the waves till the setting sun.

Casting our wishes on tides that do sway,
In our heart-shaped world, we'll laugh and play.
Every grain of sand holds a memory made,
In this slapstick saga, we're never dismayed.

With each goofy picture, a story unfolds,
Our seaside moments, worth more than gold.
We splash like kids, with pure joy to behold,
In our heartfelt horizon, warmth takes hold.

So hand me your heart, let's dream in the sky,
In this whimsical journey, we'll always fly.
With laughter as waves, and love as our guide,
On this sandy shore, we'll forever abide!

Interwoven Journeys

Two hearts set sail on a whim,
With snacks and laughs, the lights grow dim.
They trip on dreams like clumsy feet,
With every stumble, they find the beat.

In crowded buses, they share a seat,
Trading tales of a bumpy street.
The mismatched socks and chocolate stains,
Mark the joy wrapping around their veins.

Laughter echoes in the quiet night,
As shared ice cream shows their delight.
Two lives woven in a silly thread,
Whispering secrets that dance in their head.

The map's a doodle, but who cares where?
With every giggle, they fill the air.
Their journey's less about the end,
And more about the fun they send.

Cherished Footsteps

Two pairs of shoes kick up the dust,
In silly steps, it's love they trust.
Each footprint a tale of where they've been,
Like comedians on a stage, they grin.

Sidewalk chalk and goofy signs,
They scribble dreams that dance in lines.
The world their canvas, laughter flows,
Painting hearts where no one knows.

Puddles jumped, a splash and scream,
Behind each smile, a shared daydream.
With donut crumbs upon their cheeks,
Their silly banter is what love seeks.

In every café, they order strange,
Mixing flavors, they laugh at change.
Sweet notes linger in their playful chase,
Together they've found their happy place.

Harmonious Connections

A kazoo played in perfect tune,
With goofy dances that make them swoon.
Silly duets on a makeshift stage,
Gathering giggles with every page.

Twinkling lights in a sock puppet show,
Sharing secrets only they know.
A pair of misfits in a world so wide,
Creating chaos with hearts open wide.

Banana peels make the best slips,
In this adventure called silent trips.
Each spilled drink's a tale to tell,
That laughter lingers, casting its spell.

With hearts like bubbles that float and sway,
Guided by joy, they giggle away.
In this dance of clumsy delight,
Their bond transforms the day into night.

The Echo of Affection

In the kitchen, they cook with flair,
Throwing flour around like they don't care.
Each ingredient a pinch of fun,
One twirls the whisk while the other comes undone.

Dance parties on the living room floor,
With socks for slippers, they spin and soar.
Singing off-key, they let it out,
Every silly sound, a joyful shout.

The oops that follow are always sweet,
As they mix their laughter with life's heartbeat.
In this rhythm of giggles and glee,
Their affection blooms like a wild, crazy tree.

Amidst missed hugs and playful jests,
They find their bond in silly quests.
In the echoes of fun, love takes flight,
Celebrating quirks, they shine so bright.

A Tapestry of Tenderness

In a garden where giggles bloom,
Silly faces chase away the gloom.
With each lunch date, laughter's the feast,
Two hearts dance, not wanting to cease.

We twirl like socks in the dryer's spin,
Sharing secrets and ice cream, oh what a win!
Every wink and nudge is our silly art,
Crafting joy with a chuckle, a true sweetheart.

My coffee spills, a lovely clear sign,
Just means a splatter of your love on mine.
From wild adventures to quiet chats,
This silly love, oh, how it flatters and spats!

In a tapestry woven with quirks so grand,
Life's full of giggles, hand in hand.
With each mishap, cheers echo bright,
Together we're one hilarious delight.

The Serenity of Union

In a hammock strung tight between trees,
We rock back and forth, the soft summer breeze.
With mismatched socks and a giggly gaze,
Every moment brings laughter in waves.

Picnics spread out with snacks out of line,
Who knew a sandwich could be so divine?
With ants in a line and crumbs at our feet,
We laugh until we feel love's sweet heartbeat.

Sharing glances over spilled lemonade,
How quickly a mess becomes a fun charade.
We toast with a wink, our glasses all high,
Here's to love that makes our spirits fly!

In every sneeze or silly little fight,
We find a charm that feels just right.
United in laughter, our hearts are in sync,
Creating a union that's stronger, I think.

Gentle Waves of Care

On the beach where the sea meets the sand,
We chase waves, hand in hand, it's so grand.
With a splash and a laugh, we dance in the foam,
Among the waves, we feel right at home.

Wet towels and sunscreen, a comical sight,
Mixing up flip-flops, oh, what a delight!
Ice cream drips down as we giggle and smile,
In our sandy castle, we'll linger awhile.

With a sunburned nose and a goofy grin,
Who knew the beach could spark such a win?
In sandcastle forts, our laughter will soar,
Each gentle wave brings us back for more.

Sharing seashells and tales, from dusk until dawn,
Creating memories that live on and on.
Among gentle waves and whispers of care,
We find joy in moments, a love we can share.

The Oasis of Warmth

In a cozy café with cookies galore,
We sip our hot drinks while laughter will pour.
Your jokes are like sunshine; they brighten my day,
In our little oasis, we find our own way.

With sugar on our lips and crumbs in our hair,
We dance on the tables without a single care.
A game of charades leads to silly designs,
Every laugh shared is a treasure that shines.

In this snug little nook, our hearts intertwine,
With playful banter so easy, divine.
You spill your cocoa; I let out a cheer,
In our oasis of warmth, we conquer all fear.

Every moment with you is a soft, tender beat,
In our world of giggles, we can't be beat.
With cushions of laughter and warmth in our chest,
In this playful paradise, we feel truly blessed.

Beneath Shared Stars

Under twinkling lights we meet,
Pizza crumbs are our heart's treat.
Laughter echoes through the night,
Who knew love could be this bright?

Dancing shadows on the floor,
Stumbling, knocking at the door.
Each awkward step, a little gaffe,
Moments cherished, shared, and daft.

In our jokes, a silly spree,
Tangled up like spaghetti.
With every fall, we find our way,
Together, come what may.

So here's to us, the funny pair,
Weighing jokes beyond compare.
Beneath the stars, our hearts will stay,
In this wacky, loving play.

Flourishing Together

In the garden, we both dig,
Planting smiles, they grow real big.
Watered by our giggles' cheer,
Blossoms bloom, the world seems queer.

Frolicking with worms and dirt,
You joked, 'dresses won't quite work!'
Yet in the chaos, we find grace,
Love is bright, it holds its place.

Sunshine through the leafy green,
Chasing bugs, oh what a scene!
With every weed we pull and sway,
Our love sends roots in wild display.

So let's keep tending this sweet plot,
A garden bursting with all we've got.
Through laughter, tears, and gooey pie,
We flourish deep, just you and I.

Bliss Beneath the Surface

Underneath the waves we glide,
Finding joy on love's wild ride.
Splashing with our goofy grace,
Fish are laughing at our race.

With goggles that don't quite fit,
Sinking, floating, we commit.
Each bubble sends a secret cheer,
Who knew love could be so dear?

Diving deep, we lose our fears,
Swapping tales amidst the tears.
Coral castles, oh how grand,
In this sea, we take a stand.

Emerging with the sun's bright glow,
Stranded, yes, but we won't go.
Bliss beneath the surface lies,
In laughter's depths, our heart's prize.

A Garden of Kindness

In our patch, a bustling crew,
Bees and butterflies tabby blue.
We plant seeds of silly things,
Joyful laughter, love it brings.

Tending rows of quirky blooms,
Whiskers tickling, banish glooms.
Every petal, every vine,
Brings to life a love divine.

With watering cans and muddy paws,
Making vows without the flaws.
Each garden gnome gives us cheer,
In this opera, loud and clear.

A harvest full of baked delights,
Cookies flying on movie nights.
In kindness, we will always thrive,
In this garden, we come alive.

Whirlwind Embrace

In a dance of socks and shoes,
We twirl in chaos, laughs ensue.
With every spin, we trip and fall,
But oh, it's worth it, after all!

Your quirks ignite my silly grin,
Like mustard stains on my old chin.
For every giggle, there's a kiss,
In our mad world, chaos is bliss!

A spaghetti fight, just for fun,
We dodge the sauce, let's start to run!
With slippery noodles, it's a race,
In our goofy world, we find our place.

Through tickles, jests, and playful quirks,
We'll tackle life and all its perks.
Like puppets on a string we sway,
In our whirlwind, let laughter play.

Dappled Shade of Togetherness

In leaf-specked afternoons so bright,
We share our snacks, a pure delight.
Your lemonade's too sweet, you see,
But sip it down; it's love from me!

We hide from sun in laughter's shade,
With ants invading our charade.
Each joke a nut, each pun a seed,
Together we plant joy, indeed!

The breeze whispers secrets untold,
As ice cream drips, our hearts are bold.
In dappled shade, we skip and sway,
With sticky fingers, we find our way.

Through silly hats and wobbly chairs,
We'll chase the clouds and play with flares.
In this garden of giggles, we lay,
Beneath the sun's bright golden ray.

From Me to You

A paper airplane sails through air,
It carries laughter, light, and care.
With every toss, it twists and bends,
Just like the love that never ends.

My sock drawer's a battlefield,
Yet here I stand with heart revealed.
From unkempt socks, to chocolate pie,
Each silly moment lifts us high.

With crayons drawn and hearts in bloom,
We doodle dreams within the room.
Each scribble's passion, wild and true,
In a canvas painted just for you.

So take my hand, let's make a scene,
In a world where joy is queen.
From me to you, these smiles will flow,
Like rivers of bliss, we'll surely grow.

Nourishing the Soul's Garden

In the backyard where laughter grows,
We plant our dreams among the rows.
With watering cans full of cheer,
We prune the weeds, and shed a tear!

Silly gnomes guard our little patch,
They wear our hats, a perfect match.
Each flower blooms with grins so wide,
In this garden, love's our guide.

We sprinkle jokes like seeds in soil,
And dig for laughter, not for toil.
With every giggle, sprouts arise,
A cacophony of bright surprise.

So when the sun shines down on us,
We'll dance in joy, without a fuss.
In this garden where quirks are free,
We'll grow forever, you and me!

www.ingramcontent.com/pod-product-compliance
Lightning Source LLC
Chambersburg PA
CBHW050307120526
44590CB00016B/2520